EIGHTH NOTE PUBLICATIONS

Three Renaissance Madrigals

Various Composers
Arranged by David Marlatt

A madrigal is a form of poetry and music which originated in Italy during the 14th century. It was sung by various numbers of unaccompanied voices. In 1588, a collection of Italian madrigals was published in England which paved the way for the English form of madrigal. They are often either lyrical songs about love or something sad or playful songs about joy, celebration or just plain having fun (tra la la la).

In this suite there are two lyrical pieces, *The Silver Swan* and *My Heart to Thee Now Makes its Plea* and a fun, energetic madrigal, *Now is the Month of Maying*.

These pieces can be performed as a set or one could be played alone or matched with other arrangements of madrigals.

ISBN: 9781771579179 COST: $15.00 DIFFICULTY RATING: Medium
CATALOG NUMBER: WWE222187 DURATION: 4:00 2 Flutes, 2 Clarinets

www.enpmusic.com

THREE RENAISSANCE MADRIGALS

THE SILVER SWAN (Orlando Gibbons)

Expressively ♩ = 66

Arranged by David Marlatt

MY HEART TO THEE NOW MAKES ITS PLEA (Orlando Di Lasso)

THREE RENAISSANCE MADRIGALS

Flute 1

THE SILVER SWAN (Orlando Gibbons)

Arranged by David Marlatt

MY HEART TO THEE NOW MAKES ITS PLEA (Orlando Di Lasso)

NOW IS THE MONTH OF MAYING (Thomas Morley)

THREE RENAISSANCE MADRIGALS

Flute 2

THE SILVER SWAN (Orlando Gibbons)

Arranged by David Marlatt

MY HEART TO THEE NOW MAKES ITS PLEA (Orlando Di Lasso)

NOW IS THE MONTH OF MAYING (Thomas Morley)

THREE RENAISSANCE MADRIGALS

Bb Clarinet 1

Arranged by David Marlatt

THE SILVER SWAN (Orlando Gibbons)

MY HEART TO THEE NOW MAKES ITS PLEA (Orlando Di Lasso)

NOW IS THE MONTH OF MAYING (Thomas Morley)

THREE RENAISSANCE MADRIGALS pg. 2

THREE RENAISSANCE MADRIGALS

Bb Clarinet 2

Arranged by David Marlatt

THE SILVER SWAN (Orlando Gibbons)

MY HEART TO THEE NOW MAKES ITS PLEA (Orlando Di Lasso)

NOW IS THE MONTH OF MAYING (Thomas Morley)

THREE RENAISSANCE MADRIGALS pg. 2

NOW IS THE MONTH OF MAYING (Thomas Morley)